Priest Lake Lovers

Poems and Prose Inspired by a Lifetime of Summers in North Idaho

TERRY ROBINSON

Bitterroot Mountain Publishing House, LLC

Priest Lake Lovers: Poems and Prose Inspired by a Lifetime of Summers in North Idaho

© 2022 Terry Robinson

Published by

Bitterroot Mountain Publishing House LLC
P.O. Box 3508, Hayden, ID 83835
Visit our website at www.BMPHmedia.com

This book is a collection of poetry based on the author's life experiences in North Idaho. The underlying stories are a mix of fiction and non-fiction, as one would expect from a memoir-like work spanning many decades. With the exception of the author's family and friends, the characters in this book are products of the author's imagination and while they may resemble actual people, they are entirely fictional.

Interior and Cover design by Jera Publishing

For questions or information regarding permission for excerpts please contact Bitterroot Mountain Publishing House at Editor@BMPHmedia.com.

ISBN: 978-1-960059-00-0 (soft cover)
ISBN: 978-1-960059-01-7 (hard cover)
ISBN: 978-1-960059-02-4 (eBook)

Library of Congress Control Number: 2022922806

Printed in the United States of America

MAP OF PRIEST LAKE

Upper Priest Lake

Thorofare

Priest Lake

Grandview Resort

Elkins Resort

Eightmile Island

Kalispell Island

Hill's Resort

Fourmile Island

Bartoo Island

Sherwood Beach
Robinson Cabin

Soldier's Creek

Outlet Resort

Priest River

Showboat Tavern
Bishop's Marina

Coolin

This book is dedicated to my parents,
Robbie and Chickie Robinson, who loved
only their family more than Priest Lake.

CONTENTS

INTRODUCTION

The title *Priest Lake Lovers* is a play on words suggesting the book is about both those who love the lake and lovers who visit the lake. I wrote the collection of poems in this book to provide the people of Priest Lake and North Idaho something unique, memorializing the extraordinary place they live and play. Something they can enjoy and share with house guests and those they care about. Over the past fifty-five years, it's been my experience that most visitors coming to the region in general and Priest Lake, in particular, are smitten by the natural beauty. Some escape the bug, but most are planning their next visit before their current trip ends.

My first visit to Priest Lake at age twelve occurred in 1967, and the impression she made on me then is as fresh as if it were only last summer. We were city folks and had just moved to Spokane from Washington, D.C. We stayed with a family who had a mining lease cabin a mile south of Hill's resort. No running water, intermittent electricity from a wrecked Renault repurposed as a generator, and a two-seater outhouse. I had read about such impoverished living conditions in school but had no idea they still existed! Yet even in the face of those inconveniences, the pull of the lake was so intense my parents acquired a waterfront lot north of Coolin the very next summer, and we built our own outhouse.

Other than my family and friends, no one can be specifically identified in this collection of poems. However, many will see themselves in one or more. Written to share my sentiments, these poems rely on artful language to elicit emotion in the reader. In a way, they are memoir, and I want you to feel what I felt at the time. The book captures my experience with Priest Lake and North Idaho from age twelve to sixty-seven. If I did a good job, readers might see themselves in the stories. Better yet, their own memories may resurface and rekindle after lying dormant for years.

The poems herein are mostly seen through the eyes of visitors. Many own second homes at the lake but are nonetheless, by and large, not permanent residents. There is a significant community of year-round residents who call Priest Lake home. Many of them work hard in the service sector to take care of those of us recreating and vacationing. Much of the work is seasonal, and some local residents struggle, particularly during the long North Idaho winters.

I didn't write this book for fortune and fame. Very few poets make a living off their poetry. Twenty percent of any royalties I receive from the book will be donated to the Priest Lake Food Bank in recognition of the need in our community. If we sell a bunch of books, the food bank will benefit, and maybe I'll get my fifteen minutes of fame!

Robinson dock in the smoke

REFLECTIONS

As Summer Ends

I first met her fifty years ago and she captured my heart. Now at the end of a busy tourist season, with kids heading back to school, once again it is just the two of us. The large boats are mostly gone, replaced by retirees and empty nesters. As I quietly slip a kayak into her waters, I feel young again. Not much changes at Priest Lake through the years: the view of the forested hillsides across the lake, the cabins and even some of the boats. It's now as it has always been locked in my memory. Many of the neighboring cabins have been in the same families for generations—like mine.

A few strokes of the paddle and I glide effortlessly to the blue-green line marking the beginning of deep water. Unknown depths and darkness lie to the left and the familiar sandy-bottom shallow water to the right. School has started and I have the lake to myself, a calm, sunny, windless day. Water so still it takes the form of a mirror reflecting the blue sky, mountains and trees—and me. I head north, slowly without purpose, taking great care to remain on the line between dark blue and light green. To the right, fish dart along the sandy bottom, to the left, darkness. This is a time to think and to reflect. I moved away many years ago and only recently returned. I had thought I was unique that way, but have learned most of my classmates left as well. Some stayed, but many pursued their dreams in distant places. I came back partly because of feeling this is where I belong. I realize now it was fine to move on. I got that part wrong.

Paddling aimlessly northward along the blue-green line, I think of how peaceful it feels to swim in her warm waters, sail on a breezy day, cruise to the upper lake, glide in a kayak and awaken each morning by her shore. This is where I am most at peace. But for me, the lake has always been a summer place. For me it will never be home, but a home away from home. Warmer climates in the winter and perhaps the sunny Colorado Rockies have a pull on me. I left two daughters in Colorado which adds tension between the states. Fortunately they fell in love with her too, and always welcome the opportunity for a summer visit.

Somehow distracted, I have veered off the line and am approaching the family beach once again. It's time to lock up and head back to town for a few days—returning soon.

Time

Time passes, life changes.
The lake is their rock,
Unchanged as the world whirls by.

An old dirt road,
In the beginning for loggers,
Now brings families to cottages.

Midweek in October,
Kids are back in school,
The cottages are mostly empty.

After supper they walk
Down the old road to the creek.
The view is unchanged for fifty years.

They walk with limping gaits;
The years have taken a toll.
Smells from the forest take him back.

Back to when they were teens,
Summers at the lake without a care.
He takes her hand as he did fifty years ago.

He can't remember when her hair turned grey;
Being with her feels as it always has—
Fresh and new and young.

Memories flood his thoughts.
From their teens to retirement,
The past flashes by—frame by frame.

How does time escape?
Summers seem woven together—a tapestry.
When did he grow old?

They stand on the bridge looking for fish,
Where they fished on their first date so very long ago.
A cold gust of autumn wind takes him by surprise,

Reminds him of their late years.
Sun falls behind the mountain—until tomorrow;
They step off the bridge and stroll home.

Soldier's Creek Bridge

Lake Cabin Limbo Land

The cabin has stood fifty years,
Shared now by brother and sister.
Mom is ninety-three,
No longer able to make the trip.

It's still hers—not theirs.
The décor and furnishings,
Clothes hung in the closet,
Visual reminders of her absence.

They maintain and repair,
For a dozen years.
Replace aged systems as they die;
Just enough to keep it alive.

More is needed, but they are large projects,
Expenses hard to justify without ownership.
A new dock, a well, a remodel—
It's not theirs to change.

She's done with the place;
Will never visit again or finance repairs.
Her children caught in limbo land.
Evaluate each repair—Band-Aid or permanent?

After all, it's her place—she's ninety-three.
It may need to be sold to provide for her care.
If sold, it would be razed for a new cottage;
Any improvements would be lost.

So they continue to measure each dollar spent,
Does it provide lasting value or immediate pleasure?
Will the investment be recovered if sold
Or have no value to a new owner?

Caught in lake cabin limbo land
With no good answers.
Repair, maintain, and cling to the dream
Of keeping it in the family.

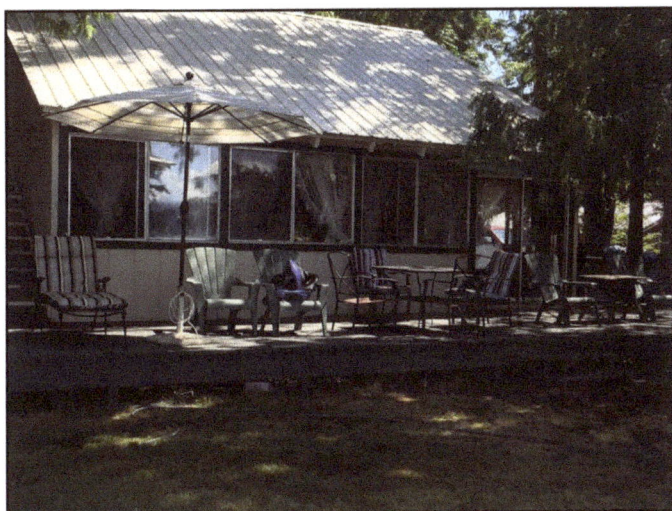

Original Robinson cabin

The Empty Slip

It's early May,
Start of boating season.
He sees it each summer,
For no apparent reason.

Boats put up for winter
Beginning early fall.
Several don't return in spring,
Resisting the warm weather call.

Some cabin owners are elderly,
Health issues in their way.
No energy to launch boats,
For young folks, child's play.

So the boat slip still stays empty,
Like a prom date who doesn't show.
For one season—or forever;
Only the family will know.

An Old Tree

The tree had lived forty years
Through summer wind, winter snow.
Once supple, green with the breeze, it swayed;
Now rigid, gray, to sandy soil it clung.

The elderly logger tied a line twenty feet up,
Pulled taut by him and a neighbor.
A young forester cut a wedge into the trunk,
Lining up the fall.

To the north, a cabin,
To the south, a power line,
To the west, a shed,
To the east, a clear path.

The forester gave his command;
His chainsaw dug into the trunk.
It creaked, moaned—leaned to the south.

Logger ran to the north, neighbor in tow,
Tension on the line as they moved—it was enough.
Cloud of dust as the tree hit the ground.

This tree once stood hard against the wind;
Now stacked in a pile, fuel for a fire.
On a path to ash.

Priest Lake Guilty Pleasure

Guilty pleasure was not new to him;
He had been touched by it before.

Twelve years earlier, he had buried his father;
The next day, he visited Priest Lake with his daughters.
It was the place dad loved most, and that feeling had been
Passed on—three generations strong.

He swam that day without a care.
Slipping into her soothing waters as the world fell
     apart around him.
Her clear water released the stress from his soul;
Water neither hot nor cold, embracing the body whole.

The feeling comes not often, but come it did the other day.
Fire-fighters from faraway places battled a blaze that
     threatened her.
Risking all to save the forest.

He slipped into her waters that afternoon,
As they fought flames on unforgiving terrain;
He soaked in her warmth.
The stress eased from his being.
Laden with guilt, suspended in her embrace, the
     serenity, the peace.

Smoke in the distance—tasted with each breath.
There he lay floating without a care;
Filled only with guilty pleasure.

My Daughter's Friend

I first met her seven years ago,
A twenty-year-old college coed
Close friends with my daughter.
Now at twenty-seven, we have shared memories.

Our personal success,
Our family tragedies,
Our growth as people,
Our Priest Lake vacations.

Why is it that some people bounce off us?
And why do others stick?
How is it that your children's friends
May in time become yours?

Maybe it was her perfume,
Maybe it was her voice,
Maybe it was our interest in the arts,
Maybe it was the memory of how I once was.

Her presence on our beach brought my youth to life:
Of when I was twenty and hopelessly in love,
Of when I was twenty-seven and dating her image—
Thirty-five years in the past.

During daylight, she represents the present.
At night, in the soft glow of flickering firelight,
She is the past. And I am twenty-seven again.

As Time Wastes Away

Time is a valuable yet wasting notion,

Too much for the young, too little for the old.

As time wastes away the enthusiasm and vigor of
our youth,

All we might hope is we are in a place we want to be.

Our family values its time at Priest Lake,

There is no greater place to be, as time wastes away.

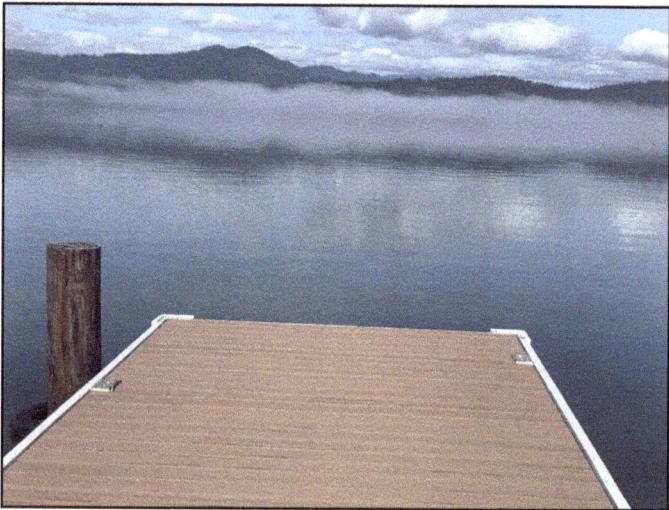

Fog over the water from Robinson's dock

The Dock

She rests peacefully in a foot of water,
One hundred feet from shore,
Elderly and water-logged—
In need of repair.

Late winter now—lake level is low.
Come spring, she will rise three feet.
The dock will float, but not well,
One storm away from beach fire kindling.

He walks across the mudflats to the dock;
Rests his tools on her moss-covered deck,
A deck of decaying, weathered cedar boards.
His attention turns to the large cedar logs below.

Cedar logs float high when first commissioned;
Twenty years in the water, and they become heavy.
The weight helps disperse large waves,
But reduces flotation as well.

He struggles to place new flotation under the dock,
Squeezed between aged logs.
The plastic-encased Styrofoam slides into place,
Secured by two galvanized lag screws.

With the determined patience of a sailor,
He will wait three weeks for the lake to fill and
    float the dock.
As mountain snow melts, the lake will rise
    inch by inch,
Letting him know if beach fire kindling looms.

THE DOGS OF
SHERWOOD BEACH

In Memory of
Sandy 1981 - 1994
and
Turner 2005 - 2019

Sandy at Fifteen

Our veterinarian gently lifts her to the table;
She lies quietly on her side gazing at me,
Reddish coat smooth from our morning brushing.

I look into my friend's eyes, sensing her alarm.
She knows this visit to the clinic is unlike the past.
She's not certain why I brought her—fears
    the unknown.

It had been my bride who wanted a dog. I
    reluctantly agreed.
We brought her home and she would never
    leave my side.

The doctor says she's giving a shot to relax her. Our life
together runs through my mind's eye—frame by frame.

Swimming in Indiana and Michigan,

Riding in the front of an aluminum fishing boat on
Moosehead Lake, her fur blowing in the
    summer breeze,

Sailing past a seal sunning himself on a rock in
    Penobscot Bay,

Chasing a ball on our Long Island Sound beach,

Playing with our girls in Lake Bridgeport,

And her favorite: visiting my parents at Priest Lake.
Running, swimming and rolling on their sandy beach.

In human years Sandy is one-hundred-five.
She no longer has the strength to do the things
    she enjoys.
Her life has been reduced to lying on her bed sleeping.
We let her in the yard to potty and watch her struggle,
Her legs no longer have the strength.

I lean on the exam table,
Run my fingers gently through her fur.
Provide comfort to her—and me.
I tell myself we're on the right path.

I look into her eyes, say softly, "Sandy, good girl."
And then, "I love you Sandy."
Lost in thought I feel a hand on my shoulder,
I face our vet and she says, "She's gone."

Overcome by grief I run from the clinic to the comfort
    of my car.
I sit alone with tears in my eyes wondering why it had
    to end this way.

Rest in peace, Sandy.

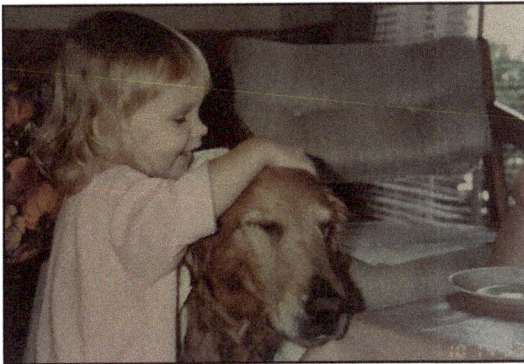

Sandy with daughter Natalie

Priest Lake Dogs

Dogs love coming to the lake,
Running and swimming,
Sunning on the beach.
There is no grander place.

City dogs arrive at the lake
To a relished freedom; no longer
Confined by a fence or held by
A leash, they are free to be dogs.

To run with each other,
To bark at the wind,
To swim for hours,
Then collapse exhausted on the beach.

Dogs of all colors and breeds
Hanging together. A pack
Bound by their love of the lake
And their humans who bring them.

Turner Arrives at His Cabin

We arrive at the cabin. Turner jumps from the truck, runs straight toward the water's edge, through the tall pines, past the startled ground squirrel—who says, "Hello." Turner hits the water with a splash, sending a mallard hen and her ducklings scurrying across the surface of the green-blue mountain lake.

We unload the weekend provisions. Turner stands in the water looking for fish. When tired of the cool water, he rolls in the warm sand, as though wrapped in a blanket.

The dinner bell rings.

Turner sprints through the beach grass to the cabin, searching for his bowl. As the sun slips behind the mountains, we brush the sand from his damp fur. He lies by the fire, falling fast asleep.

Welcome Wilson

He is young, not quite a year old,
A golden retriever named Wilson.
Sporting a reddish coat and soulful eyes
That seem to penetrate human false pretenses,
A dog who will pester any human mercilessly
Until petted to his satisfaction.
And his need for attention seems insatiable.
He's from Colorado.

Uncle Turner, who's eleven,
Leads him to the beach and the lake.
Wilson is cautious at first.
Turner wades out and calls to him,
"Come on in, the water's fine!"

Wilson's not nearly as tall as Turner.
Reaching his uncle, he's already swimming.
He swims circles around Turner with a golden smile.
When Wilson can swim no longer, he crashes
On the warm sandy beach.

Turner says, "There is no better place to be, Wilson.
Tomorrow you'll meet the other lake dogs!"

Molly the Tramp

Molly saunters onto our deck,
As is her custom while we're dining.

She's been close to Turner for most of her life,
Living in the neighboring cabin; we know her well.

Molly visits in search of handouts. If nothing
Is offered she rubs noses with Turner, then
Moves on, looking for her next victim.

Her owner lovingly calls her a tramp.
She wanders up and down the lakefront
Visiting anyone who will pay her attention.

Never staying in one spot too long,
Always returning before nightfall.

Mr. Schultz

Grandma's Schnauzer pushes
Open a screen door,
Escapes into the woods.

California dog in unfamiliar territory.
Forest begins across the dirt road,
Hundreds of square miles of wilderness.

We sound the alarm.
Form a search party:
Family and neighbors walk through the woods.
"Mr. Schultz! Mr. Schultz!"

The hours pass slowly as dusk approaches.
Someone spots a deer, another a bear.
No one spies a small grey dog.

As the sun sets over our western mountains,
A worried Grandma sits anxiously on the deck.
And like nothing happened, Mr. Schultz
Prances up to her, looking for supper.

We ring the bell, call off the search,
Signal to all,
"He's been found!"

Turner's BFF

We're cooking breakfast
And hear the lab next door call,
"Woof, woof!"

Turner runs to the screen door and asks,
"Can I go out?"

"Sure, Turner, just don't wander."

He pushes the door open with his snout,
Runs across the yard to greet Hank,
Who is searching intently for fish.

Turner joins him in the search—
Black Lab and Golden Retriever—
Pals since puppyhood.

They wander up and down the beach
Being dogs—swimming, lying in the sand,
Rolling on a dead trout.

Later they lie down and fall asleep
On Hank's front porch in the warmth
Of the morning sun.

Best friends forever.

The Boat Ride

Turner sprints ahead on the boardwalk,
I follow behind at a measured pace,
The old structure wobbles with my every step.

His nails clatter on the cedar planks—
Clickety-clack, clickety-clack.

On the beach the wild alders are in bloom,
I pause and enjoy their flowers.

I see Turner's tail wagging,
He waits impatiently at the end of the dock.

I make my way to the boat,
Drain the bilge, start the motor, free the deck lines.
Turner claims his spot in the open bow.

We start across the lake with Turner standing up front
Like a carved figurehead
On the prow of an ancient sailing ship.

At planing speed I level off.
The wind blows Turner's ears back;
His fur stands on end.

As the boat slows to dock for lunch,
Turner anxiously waits to be the first off,
Then races me to dry land.

Sadie

Our neighbor's Springer Spaniel tangles
With a porcupine. I am fetched to assist
Removing quills.

Like a fishhook lodged deep in the trout,
Those barbed quills will not surrender easily.

There are a dozen or more.
With each tug of my pliers,
Sadie squirms to be free.

How does this happen? Why does a dog
Push her snout upon the porcupine?
What was she thinking?

I free a couple, but there are many more
And now her nose is bleeding.

We put her in the truck and drive to the vet.

The Builder's Dog

Kelly turns onto our drive
To meet about building plans.
His twenty-year-old Ford pickup
Rolls to a stop with no protest.

The driver door opens,
An old cattle dog jumps out,
Lands awkwardly in the dirt,
Then disappears into the woods.

He chases squirrels and deer.
They mostly escape,
Though occasionally he gets lucky.
He has battle scars showing his successes.

The builder's daughter gave him Harley,
The active dog was too much in town. Now
He roams the North Idaho forest.

We conclude our meeting and the dog is called.
A loud shrill sound echoes through the woods
Like many high school coaches have mastered
Using the thumb and index finger of one hand.

It works. On his second pass Harley appears.
Kelly lifts him gingerly into the truck.

An elderly builder, in an ancient Ford,
With his worn out dog—off to their next stop.

Harley at Priest Lake

Alice

Turner runs to Alice, a nearly blind Schnauzer,
A hundred feet down the road.
She walks the road as though she owns it,
Even in her final years.

The sun slowly slips behind a mountain,
Casting long shadows from tall pines.
Forest sounds shift from day to night.
Leaves rustle as a small animal passes,
The Hoot Owl cries, "Who, who."

Alice's owner sips red wine
From an oversize crystal glass
As the dogs share stories of their day.

Alice says, "It's bedtime."

Turner wonders how long it will be
Until he can no longer
Take walks down the dirt road
Or stay awake for the bonfire.

Turner says, "Goodnight."
Then walks toward the beach
And the fire his kids have started.

Alice says, "See you tomorrow."
And turns toward home and her bed.

Winston

Bounding around the corner
Comes a deer or small pony,
Racing directly toward us.

No, wait …

It's Winston, a Great Dane puppy
Who appears to be four feet tall.
He lives down the beach,
He's run into us before.

We find it unnerving,
A large dog charging up to us.
His owners call him back with no success.
He's more interested in greeting Turner.

After a brief pause to sniff us, he's off again,
Galloping down the dirt road toward
The creek to get a drink of water.

Ace

It's only natural for dogs
To roam free from the leash.

Ace takes the vanguard, running loose
Down the dirt road. Bruce walks briskly
To keep pace with his grandson's poodle.

The lawyer commands Ace to return,
Which in his own time he does.
Tame to the untrained eye,
His heart beats to wild drums within.

And we should not impede nature,
Dogs should be allowed to run free.

He runs through the woods,
Jumping over the fallen birch,
Scurrying beneath low pine limbs.

A spirit released from the city
And set loose in the forest.
A soul both untamed and domesticated
In the same body.

Oh, how he longs for his cabin,
While cooped up in the city.

Oh, how he anticipates the weekend ride,
Back to paradise, back to freedom.

Tullamore and Finnegan

We see them most summer weekends
On our morning walk. Two large
Golden Retrievers running free.

Tullamore and Finnegan swim across the nearby creek.
They run to Turner and me, shaking water everywhere.
Their golden tails wag wildly.

The two surround Turner, rubbing against him.
They say, "Good morning!"

The owners are friendly and extroverted,
On par with their hounds.
Perhaps this is an Irish custom—
The wet dog greeting.

These are heavy thoughts. I love dogs.
I'll leave it to another to complain,
Should they have a mind to do so.

Exercising the Labs

It's August. Morning sun warms
The lake to a comfortable level.
The change is gradual
Like the teapot on a range
Heating water to a boil.

I step onto the lawn and watch
A kayak heading my way with
Two objects swimming close behind.
Walking to the end of the dock,
I see two dogs following the paddler.

I recognize the family as Scott,
A neighbor down the beach,
And his two labs, Gunner and Gauge.

They pass by; I raise my mug in salute
To morning workouts
And those who partake in them.
Scott waves and yells, "They need exercise!"

In a bit they pass me again headed home.
The older lab, with the gray face, falls behind,
Swims for the beach well short of their cabin.

Like grandpa on the morning family run,
He gradually slows, finishes at his own pace.

Wilson on Robinson family beach

ROMANCE

Dock Girl

They stopped for gas not so long ago,
Served by gas dock girl, golden skin aglow.

He pumped gas at a resort forty years ago or more,
Where her mother once had worked summer of
    seventy-four.

He looked into her eyes—it was her mother he saw;
He hid a blush, holding a hat against his jaw.

His wife inquired what could possibly be wrong;
Just old memories, my dear—like a favorite song.

Bishop's Marina gas dock

Priest Lake Morning Fog

Early morning, tea time,
He gazes toward the dock.
A kayak glides silently from the fog—
Could it be?

She steps onto the dock,
Filtered sunlight on her long soft hair;
An open, welcoming smile brings back
The memory of her perfume.

She waves her hand;
He lifts his in return and sips his tea.
Like the girl, the vision fades,
Sixty now—not sixteen.

Morning fog lifts from the lake;
He rises from his chair,
Makes his way to the kitchen,
Wonders what became of her.

The Ghost of Girlfriends Past

He opens the door and walks in.
It's spring, and time to open the cabin
For another season of quiet reflection,
Looking over a serene mountain lake.

For fifty years he has followed the same routine,
As he prepares the family property for summer weekends
Of those much younger than him—
Some not yet conceived.

He scans the living room and kitchen;
Nothing has changed in decades,
Some new carpet, paint,
Furniture replaced an item at a time.

His eyes shift to the loft—
The loft where he experienced
Puppy love, first love, lasting love.
The explosion following the joining of two.

Married now for thirty-five years,
He sees his college girlfriend on the balcony
As though it were yesterday.
Takes him back in time.

She stands at the top of the stairs
Wearing a yellow bikini
Showing enough to please him,
Covering enough to please his mother.

She moves gracefully down the stairs
One seductive step at a time,
Her eyes locked on his,
His wandering all over her body.

He knew he had lost the battle,
Would follow her wherever
The small patch of yellow fabric led,
Some skin, a smile and he was a puddle of pity.

Each spring as he enters the cabin
For the first time,
The ghost presents herself,
The ghost of girlfriends past.

Inside Robinson original cabin

Midwest Romance

Rendezvous in Chicago,
From Michigan
And Indiana,
A long distance romance.

Fly to Spokane,
Drive to Priest Lake
To meet his family—
The place he loves.

Upper Priest by boat,
A secluded cove,
Sandy beach, warm water,
Blue sky and sun.

Blanket spread on the sand—
Picnic, a glass of wine.
A meal, then swim—
Without suits.

Lake passion,
Wet skin covered in baby oil.
Love consummated
On virgin sand.

Was she smitten?
Did she love the lake?
He will return one day—
Will she?

Summer Love of '74

Liberty Lake lunch counter,
Silky blonde hair falling halfway down her back.
Halter top, frayed cutoffs,
Sunlight reflects off her hair, catches his eye.

Watches through the café window;
Steps through the door.
Tall, muscular and shirtless,
Reddish-brown hair, lightened by the sun.

Orders a burger—with a smile.
Small talk, banter, makes her laugh.
She feels happy again,
Agrees to meet after work.

Two lake people,
She on the rebound looking for romance,
For him a summer fling.
Pulled together by selfish needs and a smile.

Sharing weekends at family cabins,
With her family on Coeur d'Alene
And his on Priest—
Inseparable.

Weekdays working in town,
Parents on holiday out of town.
Left alone—passion runs high.
Sleeping over, sleeping in,
Lazy mornings planning futures together.

Role-playing adults, yet only eighteen.
She's excited with college beginning,
He's falling in love—forever.

College begins—
New friends, distractions—
He drops out, moves nearby.
She pulls away,
He can't hold on.

Forty years gone by, still lake people.
She at Coeur d'Alene,
He at Priest,
Her picture, the memory,
Held dear in a drawer.

Girl jumping off Robinson dock

A Teen's Lake Romance

A sunny August day,
He will head to the lake
After picking up his new girlfriend.

Sandals and shorts,
Tan and shirtless,
Backpack in the trunk.

Drives to her parent's home.
Long bronze legs, blue eyes, blond hair,
She's tailor-made for the lake.

North on the highway,
Left at the light in town—
Ninety minutes of scenic vistas.

Top down on the MG.
She holds his hand, stroking him with her thumb;
Wearing a scarf, her long hair still flails in the wind.

His family is waiting at the cabin.
He wonders how he will be alone with her,
The anticipation and excitement are palpable.

Both seventeen and not a care,
Spending the night with his family—
His mind races with sexual innuendo.

He's been with her before,
Felt the heated passion of her body,
Desires her this night again.

With family around it will be difficult—
And maybe too risky.
Slows the car as they approach the cabin.

The sun warms his shoulders;
Her touch puts him at ease.
Pulls the parking brake hard.

He leans over and kisses her.
She looks at him puzzled;
He accepts the futility of anything more risqué

Than the pleasure of her lips this night.
His parents will guard her perceived chastity
As they would his sister's.

Priest Lake fire pit

Never Thought About Her That Way

Neighbors in town and at the lake,
He was eleven when they met;
She was nine. Friends with her brother,
Never thought about her.

At the lake she was always near him,
Wanting to be included,
Crushing on an older boy,
Never thought about her that way.

As summers passed, they grew older.
He learned to drive—she rode along.
Could have parked but didn't,
Never thought about her that way.

Swimming off the island beach,
Subtle changes—hormones raged.
His interest grew—hers never faltered;
Began to think about her that way.

Quiet walks at the lake,
Along beaches, abandoned roads.
A school dance, their romance grew,
It was—that way.

Different schools pulled them apart.
Parents concerned—too young.
And yet it had grown too late,
He thought about her that way.

The Bonfire

Spread through the grapevine,
Bonfire at the resort.
It's where the action is,
Where the girls are.

Ride a ten-speed on dirt roads,
Arrive at sunset
Ready to party,
Dressed for the evening.

Guys wear jeans, t-shirts;
Girls dress in cutoffs, bikini tops.
Chilled mountain air of early summer;
Mix of local and summer kids.

Darkness quietly embraces the night air;
Courtship rituals begin in earnest.
Teens flow from group to group;
Bounce off each other like billiard balls.

He speaks to a girl—she smiles,
Looks across the fire to another guy.
He moves along to a new prospect,
Time is limited.

Cut one from the herd,
Sweet talk her into moving a few feet away—
Away from the security of the fire.
Caught between firelight and darkness, entranced by
      his charm.

Close enough to see others;
Far enough they can't be seen.
Cloaked in near darkness,
Lying on the sand.

Touching one another—with passion
And purpose. Making out
Not much more,
Risk of discovery too great.

Clock strikes midnight;
Parents wander down to the fire
To retrieve their children.
A lonely ride home.

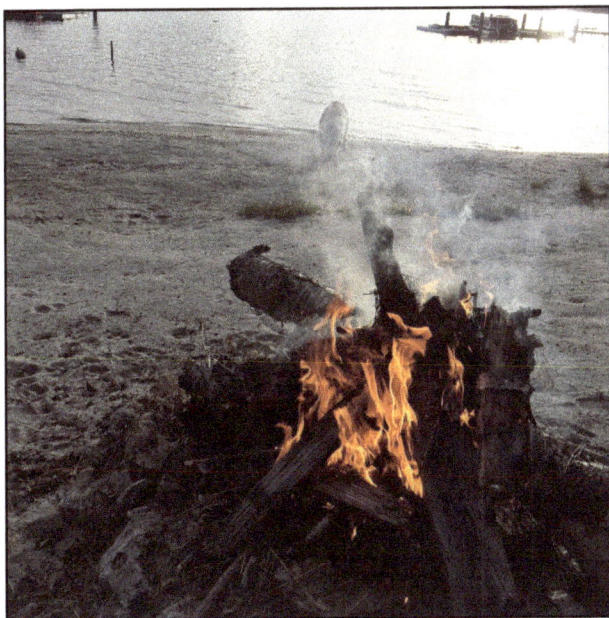

Beach fire on Robinson family beach

Girl Next-door

They were lake kids,
Growing up together,
A summer at a time.
Spending weekends at their cabins.

When they first met
She was eleven.
By fifteen he barely remembered,
She'd blossomed.

Swimming, sailing,
Beach fires following sunsets.
Labor Day lingered—time for goodbyes.
A first kiss—then wait another winter.

From different towns,
Time passed slowly.
Summer arrived one last time;
His flame still burned bright.

Sweet sixteen,
The girl next-door,
His drum beat quicker—ready to explore,
Try new things.

Trips down dirt roads,
Boat rides to secluded bays.
Spending time together—alone—
New feelings and sensations.

The warmth of her skin,
The softness of her hair,
The touch of her hand,
The taste of her kiss.

It's a memory now;
They sold their cabin—
Moved away,
Left him behind.

Elkins Resort cabin

An Old Houseboat

An old houseboat out of fuel,
Teen girl down the beach
Wanted to go for a sunset cruise.

She had watched past voyages unfold from her cabin.
Tiki torches lit, soft music playing,
Motoring slowly along the shoreline, serenading
    cabins passed.

He had watched her for weeks, desired her,
Wanted to win her affection,
Get her alone on the lake.

His father's boat had a full tank.
In a crime of passion,
He siphoned the needed fuel.

The evening was saved,
Girl was amorous,
He had his way with her.

Come morning, he was rousted from bed.
Confronted by an empty fuel tank held by his father,
A confession came quickly.

Punishment for the day:
Cleaning up a back lot in the hot sun.
He worked hard, sweat ran from his body—his
    eyes smiled.

She Loved the Lake

They met in school,
Had much in common—
School, friends, skiing
And Priest Lake.

Nothing serious—friendly banter,
Teenage flirtation, little more.
She helped him with writing,
He took her to prom.

Years later what remains?
Memories.
Lazy summers at the lake,
The pull to return soon.

Sunset at Priest Lake from Robinson family beach

Déjà Vu

Memories from the past
Rush through him
Each time he passes by
The Liberty Lake exit.

Visions of young love
Not meant to be,
Torn from a willing heart
Not fully embraced.

Lacking the sharp pain
Of a cut or break,
More like the dull ache
Of emptiness—loneliness,

Like tentacles from a creature
Reaching out from the lake,
Encircling his heart and
Twisting until he submits

To her image,
In his mind,
Emptying his body
Of all emotion.

Forty years gone by.
Likely lost her looks, as has he.
Gone would be the long blond hair
Gently falling off her shoulders.

The slender body of her youth
Will have given way to middle age
And a sensible hairdo
Barely hiding her neck.

Yet passion still burns,
Rekindled by the sign
Each time he passes by
Leaving him empty inside.

Eerie picture of Priest Lake

SAILING

Sailing's Inner Peace

It has been said there is a simple difference between a power boater and a sailor. When the power boater runs aground on a sandbar he puts it in reverse and powers back to open water. A sailor in a similar predicament prepares a cheese tray, opens a bottle of wine and waits patiently for the tide to return and free his vessel. For a power boater everything is about the destination; for the sailor it's the journey that matters.

I sail mostly on a scenic body of water in North Idaho known as Priest Lake. Please understand there are better lakes for sailing. The wind is often unpredictable due to the surrounding mountains. It can be very still for days on end during the summer. But this is the lake I fell for and I accept her for who she is. Some weekends I go through the process of freeing my boat from her mooring and relocating her to the dock. I prepare the sails, lines and other equipment for a sail that never happens. Some days there just is no wind. On Sunday evening I reverse the process and return her to her mooring. This amuses my wife to no end, "All you ever do is move that boat back and forth and adjust things – do you really enjoy that?" I answer in a word, "Yes."

I enjoy it because when the wind is up and the sun is out, within ten minutes I can be sailing. For me there is nothing as peaceful as cruising under full sail in a light breeze. As I cruise parallel with the beach one hundred yards off shore, between Four Mile Island and Coolin, I can hear dogs barking, bits and pieces of conversations and the sound of the water. Always, you hear the sound of the water. Sailing, you not only see the waves coming but you hear them as well. As each bluish-green wave crests, you can hear the sound of the white water falling from the wave's uppermost reach, marking its forward progress. You hear the wind. The sound of the wind moving through your sails is tuned in the same way you would tune a wind ensemble. Loud fluttering noise, pull the rudder slightly into the wind or fall off a degree and the pitch of the sound changes. Or adjust the sheet and listen. I have had a disk problem in my neck for years, making it difficult to look up the mast. Most of my sailing adjustments are made based on the feel of the wind on my face and the sound of her sails. While a disability for some, for me it is a blessing. Relying on those senses puts me at one with my lady.

Sailing is an acquired skill. What draws people to sailing in part is that you get better every time you sail. I started learning as a boy at scout camp and my education continues fifty years later. Each time I return to shore I feel like I've learned something new about my boat and more importantly, myself. It's nearly February now; it won't be long and I will be breaking water in a new season. And I am ready.

The Author sailing in Coolin Bay

Sailing Sandy

It was time, a summer day on Priest Lake.
The wind blew strong from the south-west.
Sandy looked lonely in the shed; I had rigged her the
    week before.
There was no wind then; she had to wait her turn.

Sailors must be patient and pick their moments.
Today I raise her sail, fluttering in the breeze,
Slip on a life-vest, swimsuit, boat shoes and sun screen.
On a thirteen foot boat you will get wet.

She is light on her feet, weighing one hundred
    twenty pounds.
A planing hull designed for speed, the speed
    of the wind.
A delicate lady, holding twice her weight in
    human ballast.

I've sailed larger, slower boats for many years.
Some days you need to go fast, push yourself to the
    edge and beyond.
Be a kid once more;
The splashing, the noise, the heeling, the rush,
    the dumping.

I know what is in store for me and cannot wait.
As I push off the dock the wind fills her sail;
She feels alive again on the open water, free
    from the shed.

We run hard upwind heeled at forty degrees,
Tacking alternating courses as we make our way south
    to Coolin.
It is hard work but she points well.

Making Coolin, we come about and run with the wind
    to the north.
Her planing hull rises from the water; we are
    screaming downwind.
As we race past our mooring, I see people on docks
    and the beach.

Feeling cocky, I turn back into the wind
Plotting a course toward the shore.
We are heeled over fifty degrees;
Water rushes over the leeward gunwale onto my feet—
Feet secured by the hiking strap.

Two-hundred-forty pounds hanging over the side
    keeping her upright.
We sail in an unstable balance between control
    and insanity.
No, we have crossed the line to insanity;
A gust or a lull and I will be in the water.

I see our neighbor the Professor.
He has placed his book on the dock and is observing
    us closely.
I plot my course directly to him three
        hundred feet out.
As distance erases, a group of people gather on a
        nearby dock, taking in my show.
I relax the tiller, falling off a few degrees, heading
        directly toward them.

We pass the blue-green line marking the
        shallow water.
Heeled as she is, we only draft a foot.
We are now less than one hundred feet from my
        spectators,
They are watching and wondering.
Will he turn soon?

I must get closer, close enough that they see my age—
A guy near retirement, an exhibitionist,
A young in spirit old man.
I need to recognize their faces and they mine.

Heart pounding, distance closing—
Now!
Instinctively, I release the sheet turning hard
        into the wind.
I duck as the boom swings by.
She comes to a complete stop, sail flapping wildly
        thirty feet from my spectators.

In an instant her sail fills, we heel over and are under
way once more.
When performed well the maneuver resembles a
choreographed ballet *on* water;
If done poorly the sailor is a spectacle *in* the water.
This day it goes well.

As I glance over her stern, the gallery applauds;
The professor picks up his book.
I seek the next thrill.
That's the way it is … sailing Sandy.

Author's sailboat Sandy on Robinson family beach

Summer Afternoon at Three

Summer afternoon at three,
Breeze builds from the south,
Steady like the trade winds.
I set my watch to them.

Sunny, warm—blowing hard.
Time to take to the open water
In a sailing dinghy rigged for one.

I drag the old boat across a sandy beach,
Ready her at the water's edge,
Hoist the main, attach the rudder.

Double check the lines,
Shove off the beach;
I step gingerly into her center,
As if she may tip over.

My weight disrupts her balance—
Spar swings wildly to one side,
Tiller shifts out of reach,
Sail flaps violently.

I reclaim the tiller,
Pull the main sheet in and with it the boom.
She begins to move with the wind
Like a leaf fluttering in a fall breeze.

Now in control, I tighten the main,
Guide her into heavy air.
She heels and we're off!
We easily clear nearby docks.

My course is set
To nowhere in particular.
Up the shoreline a nautical mile or two,
Then run with the wind—retracing our steps.

The breeze turns light but steady;
I cleat the lines
And sit low in the cockpit.
My feet dangle over the gunwale.

I cruise past cabins and docks,
One hundred feet away.
Listen to quiet sounds,
Wind, waves—voices on shore.

I can make out their faces
And hear them speaking.
The words are muffled
Like a familiar song in a foreign language.

Sailing small boats is hard work;
In an hour I've had my fill.
Time to put another day to bed,
Secure my vessel until tomorrow.

Tomorrow ... summer afternoon at three.

Morning Sail

Mountain forest on fire,
Smoke drifting to the lake,
Clinging to early morning fog.

Sailing without instruments,
Searching the distance
For a landmark, another boat,
Any hint on position.

She cuts silently through blue water.
Subtle sounds of sailing—
A breeze luffing her sails,
Waves lapping gently against her hull.

Morning sun burning off the fog
Leaves behind only smoke;
Smoke illuminated by sun rays
Forming a halo around my ship.

Our path now clear, we come about,
Point hard into the wind.
She heels and heads for her mooring.

Bishop's Marina

She stood peacefully in Coolin Bay for generations,
Stately and secure against the wind,
A refuge from any storm,
Rising plank by plank on a foundation of wood pilings
Pounded into the lakebed.

Whitewashed and faded,
A hopeful beacon for sailors rounding the point
    from Hill's,
Or running through the channel at Four Mile,
Or passing Bartoo Island.

The sight of her brought comfort and hope.
During storms, her breakwater promised calm;
A two-story building anchored majestically to
    the beach,
With docks protected beneath.

A much-loved historic structure,
She should have been protected and preserved.
I watched Bishop's from our dock in summers as a
    child two miles to the south.
I watched her dismantled during winter as an adult
From Colorado via webcam.

One heartbreaking plank at a time,
Each reluctant piling pulled from the lakebed,
Continuing until there was nothing.

Nothing but my memories:
Of playing on her docks as a kid,
Of buying fuel as a teen,
Of sharing her secrets with my children.

They visited her and ran on her docks,
Sensed her history and the mystery of her past.
What might have been hiding in her loft?
Oh, the secrets she held.

Could she have been saved?
Had she been neglected for too long?
We will never know—
She's gone.

.

SEASONS

Spring Chill

Spring is not kind to him—
Rain, snow and wind,
Moisture hangs in the air
Soaking everything.

Left unheated for a week,
The cabin is damp and cold.
A cold that permeates the interior,
His recliner has chilled to its core.

A hard to shake, persistent cold
Draws heat from his body as he waits,
Leaves him feeling weak and achy.

A fire burns in a stone fireplace.
Ancient baseboard heaters turn on,
Mixing the aroma of burning wood
With burning dust.

Flames light up the room, still it takes time,
Time for the wood floor and furniture fabric
To absorb heat from the fire;
Time for the cookware and hand towels
To once again feel warm to the touch.

As the cabin warms and comes to life,
He sits comfortably in his overstuffed chair with a book.
Only then does he hear the rain on the metal roof—
Soothing, peaceful, reassuring.

As darkness falls he adds a log from the hearth.
He pours a glass of wine and drifts off to the music of
the pattering rain,
Embraced by the warmth of the fire he created.

Cabin at Priest Lake with chair by fireplace

Seasons

Fall laid darkness across the north lake country;
He moved south to a place with less snow.
Daylight hours were few—and precious—during
    winter months;
Come spring he rediscovered the warmth of the sun.

Spring transitions to summer, then to fall, and
    finally winter.
He doesn't count years, rather summers at the lake.

Making his way there each spring he remembers
    years past,
Each one unique, memorable as if birthdays of a child.

He readies for the annual journey to the lake
like Native Americans planned centuries ago.
He breaks camp in the light of the new sun,
Prepares to leave a land that wintered him well.

He has traveled this path for fifty springs.
Now he finds the weight heavy,
A struggle to load provisions, later unload.

As a young man, outdoor furniture, boats and toys
    emptied from the moss-covered shed quickly;
In an afternoon it was as it had been the summer before.
Now he slowly retrieves only what is needed—by
    the Fourth.

At summer's end, everything is out of the shed.
Rain on Labor Day sends an unwelcome
      reminder of fall,
Time to move summer items back to the shed
And prepare once again for the faded light of winter.

Original Robinson family boat shed

Opening the Cabin

The ice thaws, snow turns to slush,
A cold rain falls—through forty-degree air.

Winter's long—and now spring is chilled,
Yet cabin owners wonder how their places fared.

It's a Saturday in early May,
A steady stream of cars heads to Priest Lake.

Temperatures have risen enough,
Fear of frozen pipes alleviated
In the summer cottages scattered along the shoreline.

For many, the systems are old,
Turning them on is not intuitive—
Attach the foot valve to the end of the line,
Weight the pipe, drop it in the lake.

Turn one valve counter clockwise,
Then twist another clockwise,
Prime the pump,
Fill the hot water tank.

As the water begins to flow so do the dreams
Of another summer at the lake.

Original Robinson family dock

Memorial Weekend

He left for the cabin Wednesday after work,
Took time off through Tuesday,
Wanted to experience the busy weekend as the
    retired do.

It was the annual informal kickoff of lake season—
Fund raisers, boat launchings, parades and pancake
    breakfasts.
A carnival atmosphere where the population would swell
From a few hundred to a few thousand.

Thursday was dead quiet;
The day provided no hint of the change to come.
Friday afternoon the highway was choked with cars
And trucks towing boats and travel trailers.

By early evening, the masses of weekenders were
    arriving at their cabins.
He longed for the quiet of the day before; it would not
    return until Tuesday.

Reaching their destinations, kids were cut loose;
They raced down dirt roads on four-wheelers and
    dirt bikes.

Disturbing the peace; recreating in their own way.
Kids barely old enough for Kindergarten, riding
    vehicles designed for adults.

No parents in sight.
Two and three passengers on units meant for one,
Kicking up dust that drifted onto his deck.

The noise and commotion continued through
 Monday morning.
Then as quickly as they arrived, SUVs and trailers were
 loaded and headed south.

Monday evening, peace returned.
He sat on his deck and savored the quiet;
Tuesday the lake was peaceful again,
The quiet enjoyed by him and his dog.

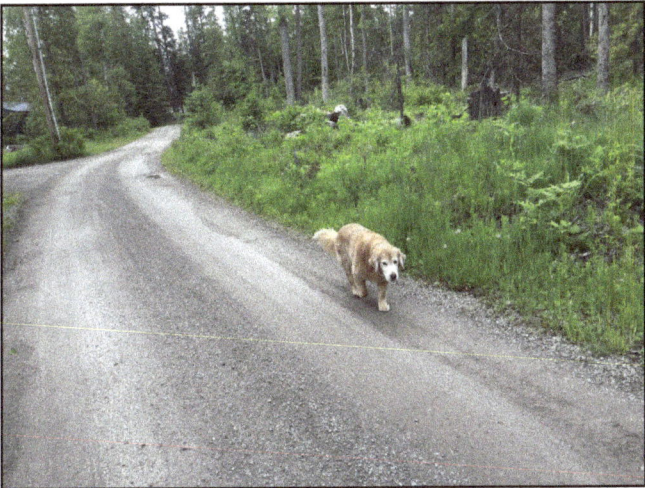

Author with Turner on Steamboat Bay Road

Welcome Summer Rain

I hung laundry, it began to rain,
Moisture we have missed for some time.
The forests surrounding our mountain lakes are dry
and on fire.

Crews have been sent from across the country to save
our woods.
We can't do it alone,
They can't do it alone,
We need help from God and today he provided.

Rain fell steadily and will give our crews the edge
they need,
Rain without lightning—a blessing.
Our community is indebted to the fire crews.
We know them a bit, through pictures on Facebook,
They look tough and dirty and hot
And fearless and strong and able.

We try to repay them in small ways—cookies, cakes,
cold drinks.
It is not enough, yet it is all we can do.
And it helps,
It helps them and it helps us feel a part of the fight.

The fire will be put out,
Crews will head for the next venue,
We will remember them,
Hope they will remember we cared.

Fall Has Arrived at the Lake

Labor Day—the unofficial end of summer,
It shouldn't be, but it is.
School will start soon
And with it a focus on other things.

The hot days of August are gone,
Replaced by the warm days of fall.
Days are shorter, water cooler,
A sense of winter is in the air.

The busy families have left,
Returned to their stressful lives in town.
During summer, they move their hectic lives to the lake;
We don't miss that they're gone.

The big powerboats are stored for winter.
The lovers of fall may peacefully paddle their kayaks.
They no longer fear being swamped by a surfboat or
        terrorized by kids on jet skis.

They paddle quietly, listening to migrating birds
And hear the sound of the water's waves.
A weakened sun warms their shoulders.

Indian summer in the north country doesn't last long;
Nights soon grow colder, lake temperatures drop.
Fireplaces are put to use.

The first freeze brings a sense of urgency;
Summer holdouts drain their pipes, winterize
     their cabins.
They prepare to follow Canadian geese south.

They hold on as long as they can;
By Halloween or early November they throw in the
     towel on another season,
Leave the lake to the hardy permanent residents.

Only to return in May.

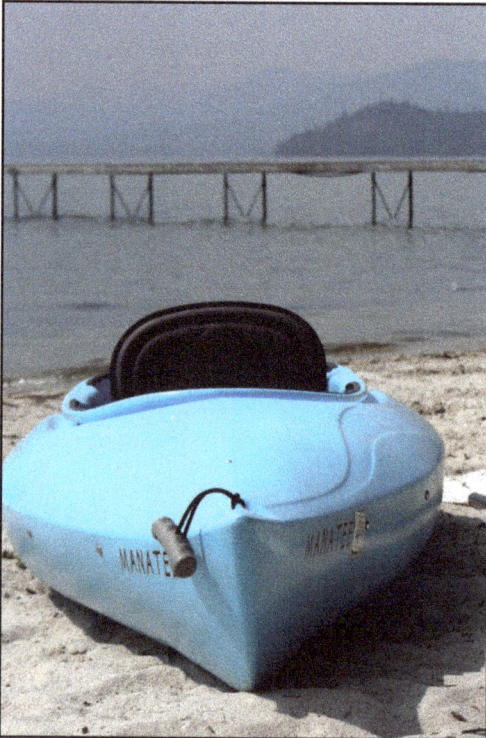

Robinson family beach

Sunrise on Sherwood Beach

Sunrise over Sundance Mountain
Streaming light into my room,
Washing across my face
Like sand on a deck
Chased by a broom.

I could sleep another hour
Into the new day;
But the sun announces
It is time to awaken
And play.

This day on Sherwood Beach
I have no plans,
Only to enjoy
Quiet reflection
On Priest Lake sands.

Winterizing

That late summer morning felt somehow different.
Might have been the early dawn darkness,
Or light fog stubbornly refusing to let go of the lake.

Most evident was the morning chill,
Not quite cold enough for a winter coat,
But enough to get the fireplace started.

A lingering and persistent damp cold.
The kind of cold where you sense the old lake cabin is
    calling it a season,
Stepping aside for fall and then winter.

Draining the water system is always a sad time,
Yet also a feeling of accomplishment—knowing the old
    place should winter well,
And be ready once again ... come spring.

Sending Linemen Into the Night

The wind abates without fanfare,
Gone as suddenly as it arrived. In its wake,
Broken poles, downed lines along the lakeshore.

Phones light up, power's off.
Dispatch calls go out,
Sending linemen into the night.

Blocked roads, wires sparking.
Safety first for the team, their mantra
'Everyone goes home tonight.'

A culture, a philosophy,
Guides all they do,
Keeps them safe.

When too tired, wet, and cold,
Foreman calls them off. Stay safe,
To work another day.

More than a job, it's a calling;
Lake residents depend on them,
Fueling their desire to serve.

The co-op feeds them, clothes them, provides tools.
They bring dedication, strength, heart,
Watch over each other through the night.

Later, power's back on. Letters trickle in to the co-op,
Many from the elderly, singing praise of their heroes—
What would our vulnerable have done?

They follow a humble creed. Carry out their mission
With quiet confidence. And a safety culture,
'Everyone goes home tonight.'

Kootenai Electric Cooperative crews after a storm

Winter Lake Visit

January, time to check on the cabin,
Winterized against cold weather
Until the warmth of spring arrives.
Clear snow from the roof, look for dangerous trees.

Dog races under way at Priest Lake,
Iditarod time trials.
Tune-up for Alaska—
'The Last Great Race on Earth.'

Siberian Huskies are the dog of choice,
Formed into packs. A pecking order
With an alpha-male lead,
Bred for competition—and the cold.

I walk through the teams,
On a break between heats,
Large cauldrons of mush, looks like chili.
Dogs barking—howling.

My golden looks out of place, out of sorts.
What does my suburban dog think of this?
Is it fear, confusion—envy?
Or perhaps he just gives thanks it isn't him.

My dog's life is different,
Chasing sticks in the lake,
Rolling in the warm summer sand.
Sleeping outdoors? Never!

Soon spring will arrive:
Days will grow longer,
Snow will be a memory,
The summer people will return.

Nell Shipman's sled dogs on the ice with Lloyd Peters

WILDLIFE

The Woodpecker

A commotion arises;
Sound filters through the pines—
A sense of urgency, panic, pain.

Four frantic children yell at their dogs;
A ten-year-old holds one back.
Spaniels after an injured bird.

Skin torn, flesh exposed, leg broken,
The woodpecker is badly injured.
Attacked earlier by a raven or another animal,
An elderly bird near journey's end.

Two neighbors arrive and set calm to the mayhem.
The retired logger speaks softly to the children,
Tells them to leave the bird alone—in peace—
That it will die by nightfall.

He would end the bird's misery if a younger man.
Nearly eighty, he senses a kindred spirit;
They are both old and travel similar paths.
He sees himself in its eyes, lacks the heart to end its life.

The second neighbor is young, has yet to face his
        mortality.
He has a kind spirit and comforts the bird,
Transfers him to an old blanket in a darkened shed
Where the woodpecker rests—in peace.

Once proud and stately, climbing the tallest trees,
Reduced now to an immobile heap of feathers.
By late evening he is gone,
Buried in the garden beneath his favorite tree.

Woodpecker at Priest Lake

Fire at Priest Lake

Lightning strikes the mountain forest.
Days pass, embers smolder,
Wind blows, a fire grows.
Summer grass bursts into flames;
Fire spreads along the forest floor,
Climbing into trees.
The scent of smoke ebbs and flows,
Drifting toward the lake.

Animals nervously sniff the air.
Sensing danger, a migration begins.
A death march where resting may bring the end.
They move east, away from danger.
Deer, elk, moose, bear, wolves, birds,
Large and small, all seek fresh air and water.

Weary and covered in soot,
They cross the highway, stunned and frightened.
Vehicles stop, providing passage.
Heads down, one foot following the other,
A parade of souls seeking safe haven.

The forest is home to wildlife;
Much of this familiar home cannot be saved.
The animals are on the move and will not soon return;
They will find a new place, a new home.

Priest Lake Sandpiper

Trimmed the grass along a beach wall,
Used a scythe to cut it down.
Saw a brown bird so small,
Heard it make a piping sound.

A long narrow beak and skinny legs,
Protecting her nest containing three eggs.
With kids and dogs, the nest was in danger;
He put up a structure to serve as a manger.

Not long after, to his delight,
Those eggs hatched and the birds took flight.
The beach is not ours, it is there to share
With lake animal friends and those in their care.

Eagle

Morning tea on the dock,
Lake embraced by thin layers of hazy fog.
Above, blue sky,
Early morning quiet, peace.

Sound of wings brushing the air,
Search the sky. Until—
They see the eagle,
High up, circling.

From her lofty height
She spots a fish,
Begins a descent,
Turns into a dive,

Talons extended,
Meets the water with a splash.
She grasps a hapless fish,
Glides just above the surface,

Begins to climb toward the sun,
Heads for her nest in a tall pine,
And then drops the fish to her eaglets,
Stands guard as they feast.

A Flock of Geese

On Bishop's gas dock,
Sound of geese honking, wings flapping,
Flying low over the pumps.

Beautiful, peaceful,
Birds in flight formation,
Passing in slow motion.

Split, splat—the moment is lost,
Bird poop on the attendant,
Buddies grab a hose to rinse him off.

It's five o'clock,
Closing time,
Laugh it off over a beer.

Geese taking flight at Priest Lake

The Hornet Hive

He needed to clear a path
Wide enough for an ATV.
Through the years the land had been improved,
Leaving no access to the beach.

He toiled beneath the hot sun.
Cleared brush and abandoned items
To make a path sixty inches wide,
Enough to drive through.

As he moved a neighbor's small boat,
He noticed hornets,
Thought little of it at the time.
Moving to the other side of the boat, he saw the hive.

The hive was large,
Size of a grapefruit.
He kept raking,
Taking care to leave the boat undisturbed.

As darkness fell he crept
Close to the hive,
Applied wasp spray,
Saturating the nest.

A large hornet climbed halfway out the opening,
It seemed to gaze at him.
The look held the question—why?
Why have you done this?

He felt a pang of guilt;
He had destroyed a nest of living creatures.
They could have done him harm,
He was right to do so—but still.

Hornet hive at Priest Lake

Boys' Fishing Trip

Four in the morning
The alarm sounds,
Fish are waiting.

Two boys, both twelve,
Barely awake,
Ready to catch breakfast.

They leave the cabin quietly,
Taking care to not slam the screen door.
Head down a path to an old dock.

Summer in north Idaho:
Morning dew, everything left outside is damp,
Ambient light steadily increasing, only forty degrees.

They climb into an aluminum boat,
Squeeze the fuel bulb.
Two pulls, the motor turns over.

Another pull and it sputters to life.
They sit in silence,
Motor idling roughly,

Each lost in his own thoughts,
Preparing tackle,
Securing rods.

One boy unties from the dock, shoves off.
His partner slips the motor into gear,
Heads for open water.

Their destination is predetermined,
Two miles to the south,
The point off the resort.

Lake flows toward the south,
Spills into the river near the resort.
Fish congregate in the bay.

In ten minutes they are there,
Drop their lines.
Within an hour they have their limit.

As they round the corner near their cabin,
Smoke wafts from the chimney,
Smell of pancakes in the air.

Fish catch at Hunt Creek near Priest Lake

FAMILY
AND FRIENDS

Old Mining Cabin

An old mining cabin south of the resort,
Family friend won the lease rights.
Though ownership was tenuous,
They made the cabin their summer home.

Family and guests shared summer weekends,
Vacations in a private bay.
A primitive existence,
Lacking modern conveniences.

Two seater outhouse, no running water,
A wood cook stove,
Intermittent power from a junked Renault
Used as a generator.

Resort luxury a mile down the road,
Yet they relaxed in the glory of their good fortune.
They after all—had a cabin,
Very few did.

Tide turned against them,
State said the mine must produce
Or our friends must vacate.
Price of silver was too low.

Our friend resisted,
Officials were angry.
Late night fire, cabin burned to the ground,
Tailings pile all that remains.

The Caretaker's Trailer

It's an oddity of sorts,
Nestled between two lake cabins.
If lake lots had covenants,
Surely it would have been removed long ago,
Yet—there are no covenants.
The caretaker's tiny ancient travel trailer remains.

Caretaker worked hard for the privilege,
Raking the owner's lot and beach each spring,
A large lot with dozens of mature trees.
Each winter wreaked havoc on the forest,
Only to be followed by the caretaker and his rake.

The owner lives in Colorado,
Has no desire to rake during his vacation.
The caretaker's uncle owns the cabin next door;
Trailer's connected to the uncle's electricity, water
        and sewer.
A complicated marriage of two families going
        back in time.

The caretaker spent summers in his uncle's cabin;
As a young boy, owner got to know him well.
Now three households weekend on two lots,
Two cabins and a small travel trailer
Straddling the property line,
Now forever blurred by long-standing family ties.

The Traveling Gnome

As his sister arrives at the lake
For two weeks each summer,
He heads to town at daybreak,
Feeling life's a bummer.

He wouldn't feel included
With such a large crowd;
He likes to feel secluded,
His family is not so loud.

So he spends two weeks away
Secluded in his Coeur d'Alene home,
Until his sister completes her stay
And he returns like a traveling gnome.

Sharing a Cabin

He drives up in the winter months,
Through sleet and snow,
To check on the lake cabin.

As spring arrives,
So do the fallen branches, leaves and needles.
A lake lot with a sandy beach—yes—
But a parcel carved from the forest.

He rakes and rakes and ….
Piles carted into the deeper forest
To waiting slash piles,
Burned to ash each winter.

As the calendar turns to June,
The mosquitoes turn thick.
He lathers on repellant,
Repairs the deck and dock and ….

He works hard each weekend
May through mid-July,
Then like the return of the hummingbirds each spring,
His sister's family arrives for two weeks—
The end of July through early August.

If the year was a watermelon
Those two weeks would be its heart,
Cut from the year, removed beyond his reach.
As the sister makes her way to the lake,
He passes her in town—at the stoplight.

On her final Sunday—they will pass again,
As he returns to the lake he loves
And begins his summer.
Come Labor Day, he will start the process
Of storing things away
And winterizing the cabin.

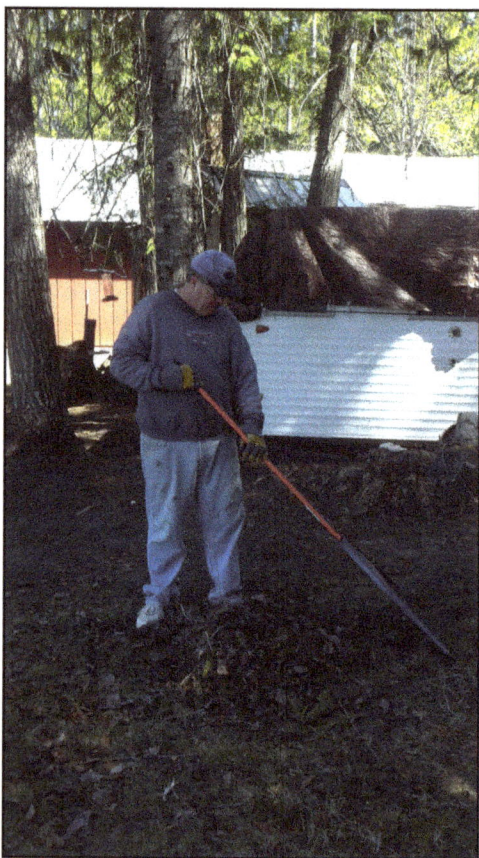

The Author raking the original Robinson family lot

My Father

Time passes, memories fade, emotions linger;
His spirit lives on.
At the lake cabin as a kid *I* did nothing.
Older now, I work hard on *his* cabin.
Reaching sixty, questions loom—
Will I be as *he* was?

I bought a truck;
To the young salesman I said,
"This cost more than my first house."
He said I sounded like *his* dad.

No, it was the voice of *my* father.
The journey to our destiny is long,
I have arrived without fanfare.
It is who *I* have become;
I am my father's image.

Anticipation

Plain empty box,
Resting on the kitchen floor
Next to the garage door.

Weekdays slowly pass; it begins to fill:
A can of tomato paste, package of noodles,
Spark plug for a fishing motor.

By Friday,
The box is full,
Provisions for the weekend.

After work he moves the box to the station wagon,
Adds luggage and family,
Heads for the lake.

College Beer Run

Five o'clock in Spokane,
Head to the lake
With a buddy.

Arrive at Sherwood Beach—the cabin—
Six-thirty;
Mom heats up a plate.

Fire up the boat,
Head south for Coolin,
Grab a beer at the Showboat.

Head west toward Outlet Resort,
Down a brew,
Visit with the owner, my former employer.

Follow the shoreline north and west to Hill's,
A bit upscale, but great ambience—
Order a tall schooner.

Next stop Elkins,
Family atmosphere,
Sit outside with a draft.

Round the bend and stop at Grandview,
Band is playing, people are dancing—
Relax with a drink, stay a while.

Closing time,
Find the boat and head to the cabin,
Avoiding islands along the way.

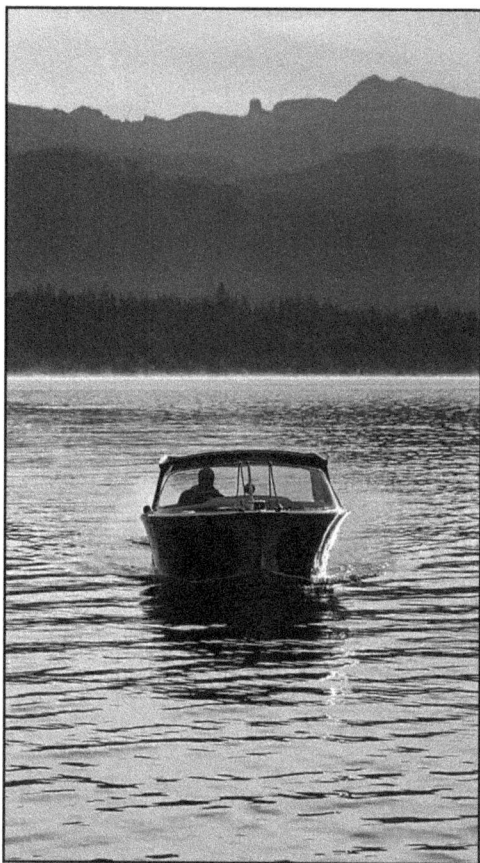

Boat on Priest Lake after sunset

The Lake's Call

Friday's here, we've earned our pay;
Head up 41, after work today.

Stop in Newport, a quick bite to eat
Enroute to the lake, where friends we'll meet.

Some drive too slow, some too fast,
We hit 57, turning north at last.

Want to reach the lake before night can fall,
A stream of Priest Lakers heeding the call.

Intersection of US 2 and State 57 in Priest River

ROAD TO RETIREMENT

Enough

My forty-something lake neighbor said, "You seem too
    young to retire."
I protested, "We work for money, when do we
    have enough?"

When I started working, I flew coach,
After a promotion, I flew first-class,
Wondered how coach people suffered through it.

I had a client with a fractional jet membership,
Cost four times first-class, but you had your own jet!
Told him he had it made.

He said, "My neighbor owns his *own* jet—*he*
    has it made."
My client went on that the neighbor wasn't satisfied
Because he knew others with larger jets.

Paycheck or golden parachute, mansion or
    mountain retreat—
Someone will always have bigger and better.

When do *we* have enough?
Where do *you* draw the line?

What to Do

Sleeping now, dreaming really,

On a wire high above life's turmoil,

Cannot hold on much longer.

Pulled from the left by the Rockies,

The kids are there, the money is better,

From the right by retirement,

Freedom and time at Priest Lake—

Time money cannot replace.

At forty, eighty seemed distant,

Now sixty, the thought frightens.

What to do?

Surrender to the allure of the lake?

Retire and be free?

Or cave to the money, toil on as a salary-man?

What to do?

Counting

In my teens it was the thrills,

In my twenties I counted honeys.

Once thirty, it was my skills,

At forty I counted monies.

Come fifty, it was days at Priest Lake,

Mornings at the cabin when I awake.

Sailboat for Sale

I have worked hard
For forty years.
Retirement is within my grasp,
Yet life is incomplete.

I love to sail, but
Haven't for many years,
Life has gotten—well—
In the way.

I searched the classifieds
For a used sailboat,
Large enough to not easily capsize,
Small enough to handle alone.

I found a nearly new vessel
Nineteen feet in length,
Displacing eleven hundred pounds,
She had never been sailed.

I asked the seller, "How can that be?"

He said his father worked hard
For forty years,
Looking forward to retirement and sailing,
He bought the boat, retired—and died.

I gave notice the very next day.

Retirement

As the sun sets on his career,
He wonders in his Sunday pew—
Will he have regrets?
Sinatra had a few.

Sunrise brings retirement,
He sits pensively on the sand
Will there be new challenges?
He seeks a guiding hand.

The lake is a special place,
A week or just the day,
Visits cherished each year—
Will it feel the same with a longer stay?

He will try to stay the summer,
His retirement's first year,
To see if he can retain the magic
Of the lake he holds so dear.

Open the cabin in spring,
Ready for guests by late May,
Pack it up in September,
After celebrating Labor Day.

CHANGES

Fifty Years of Change

Fifty years,
The feeling has changed,
Not sudden like jumping in an alpine lake,
But gradual, as if watching an ice cube melt.

In his early years Priest Lake was the working
    man's lake.
Tucked into the Selkirk Mountains of North Idaho
She was difficult to reach,
Lacked the comfortable accommodations of
    other lakes.

But it was worth the hardship.
Teachers, loggers, farmers—
They all bought land along her shore;
From the forest modest cabins emerged.

Cabins from which family legacies were born
And continue today,
Yet those families are now conflicted
By the change surrounding them.

In some change he sees good:
Paved roads, a fire station,
Modern landfill, sewer systems,
A growth in small businesses.

Not all change though—
He can't recall the day
There came a moment in time
When he longed for the past.

Paved roads brought wealthy families,
They were different than he,
Business owners, celebrities, captains of industry.
Their lives were different too.

With them came enormous lake homes,
Staffed to improve and maintain.
Dwellings occupied briefly each summer,
Then left empty, sparkling bling on a sandy beach.

They remade the community fabric in their
    own visions,
Not understanding the lake's traditions.
They replaced pancake and spaghetti feeds
With glitzy dinners and silent auctions.

It's all for a good cause; he accepts that.
And for now they share the lake amicably;
Each enjoys her in their own way,
The old-timers and the new money.

It may not always be that way.
With the closing of each small family resort,
Destruction of another old rental cabin,
They reduce access to the lake for others.

He fears the day may come
When the last of his people are gone,
Access is restricted and
The lake serves only a select few.

Teardown Cabin

For fifty years she has sat
Anchored to the land,
Above the breaking waves,
Along Sherwood Beach.

A summer cabin
Built the old fashioned way,
With beer, family and friends—
On an exposed post and beam foundation.

Time and elements take a toll
On boards exposed to weather,
Joints are weakened, wood is rotting,
Floor is no longer true.

They referred to her as a teardown,
But this is not California,
The Hamptons, Seattle, Sedona or
Other snooty enclave.

This is Priest Lake, where
McMansions rest comfortably
Next to cabins from the fifties
Or places families camp on their lots,

Until they save the money
To pour a foundation,
Drill a well, connect to the sewer
And finally build a summer cottage.

At this lake most people
Are about being *on* the lake,
Not about sitting inside a nice house
That could have been built anywhere.

So she continues to stand
And serve the families who love her,
Who will hear none of this talk
About her being a teardown.

Original Robinson Priest Lake cabin

She Was Ninety-three

A wife, mother, sister, daughter, aunt,
Grandmother and great-grandmother,
Strong and independent—a military wife—
She was ninety-three.

I was not the best teenage son,
Headed east at twenty-five
In search of fame and fortune—
Absent for thirty years.

Dad passed, and in time
I returned to the only home I knew,
Her home of fifty years—
She was ninety-three.

For the seven years before she passed
We shared every holiday—save Christmas.
Thanksgiving, birthdays, Easter, Mother's Day
Were spent making up for years lost.

Christmas was in Colorado
With our children;
Left alone, she didn't seem to mind—
She was ninety-three.

Her spirit was strong and young,
The body aged.
I drove her to see doctors, friends and funerals—
She never wanted to be a bother.

It was no bother—I was making up for lost time.
Near death with a heart rate of sixteen,
I put a med-alert in her home,
Wouldn't push the button—didn't want to be a bother.

My sisters moved mom
From her home;
Reluctantly, she relocated
To the dark side of the Cascades.

Once there, she received needed care.
No doctor could fix the emphysema or
    weakened heart.
Her family at bedside, she took a last gasping breath—
She was ninety-three.

**Chickie Robinson with Author,
his daughters and son-in-law**

Replatting the Cabin

Cabin was held in trust;
When mom passed,
It became my sister's and mine—
One-half interest each.

Two deeded lots,
Small cabin built over
The common lot line
To discourage selling.

It's been fifty years
Since our family built it,
With borrowed labor,
For a summer retreat.

Now we have options,
More correctly—choices.
Keep the property as is
Or start afresh.

Could move the cabin
To fit on just one lot,
Then build another
On the other.

Tear the old place down,
Leaving two vacant lots
To build two new abodes—
Haven't the heart for that.

It's not my decision alone,
Two must share and decide;
We use the lake differently,
Resulting in unique needs.

Lot line must be adjusted,
A survey and replat required,
With county approvals;
It feels like a committee.

Logistics are a nightmare,
May lose a summer's use
To construction timeline.
Or leave it be, use as it is,

As it's been for fifty years.
Siblings sharing an old cabin,
Maybe add a travel trailer
For grandkids and guests.

After all, it's Priest Lake in the summer—
How much time will be spent indoors?

Family Legacy

Cabin on a mountain lake,
Owned by siblings.
Felt like the day would never arrive,
Yet they always knew it would,

Bringing with it mixed blessings.
Half owners each of
A fifty-year old lake house.
Ownership vested with the passing

Of their mother who, with father,
Held the rustic, wood paneled, one bath
Home dear. Idyllic retirement embodying
Emotions from *On Golden Pond*.

Not much lasts forever,
Not parents, not buildings.
Only memories live on—
Little else survives.

The structure will come down.
Memories are in their hearts
And will remain alive within
For generations to come.

A structure is lumber and glass,
Built by following a plan.
A cabin is furnishings and memories
Built by a family living their plan.

The backhoe and dozer,
The dumpster and crew
Can't remove love from
The hearts of cabin families.

Their new cabins will replace the old.
Family legacy resides within them,
Will move seamlessly from old to new,
Anchored by a framed photo of their former
    lake home.

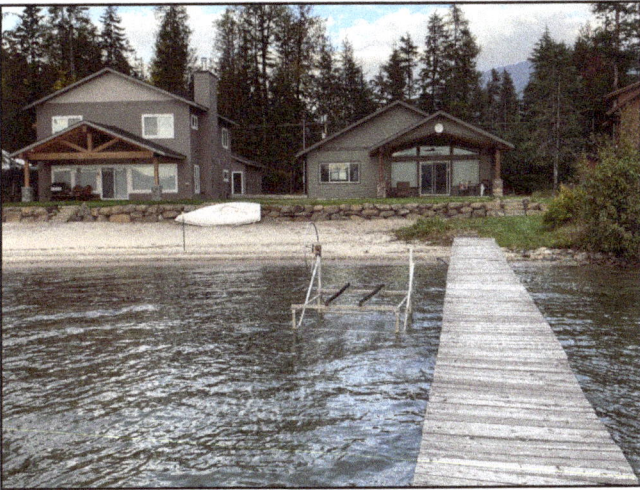

**The Author and his sister's new cabins on the
original lot**

Camp Robinson Golden Anniversary 2018

It was the golden anniversary of Camp Robinson.
Our parents purchased two lake lots
Five decades earlier on
Priest Lake's Sherwood Beach.

We spent summers working our property,
Cleared the land, framed a small cabin
With a loft above. We camped in tents on the beach
During weekends and vacations as we built.

The fourth year we moved
Into a cabin with no doors, flooring or walls—
Like a child's play fort left unfinished inside,
Lacking electricity or running water.

We added wire for power,
Pipes for plumbing, built a pump house,
Ran a water-line into the lake.
Back then we would drink the untreated water.

There were rolls of insulation and wood paneling,
Finally the hand-me-down furniture
And housewares from homes in our past.
Our parents traveled the world,
We decorated the walls with the bounty they
brought home.

It's been a hard fifty years in the North Idaho climate,
The cabin barely survived.
Post and beam foundations leave much exposed;
Weather has taken a toll.
We've done repairs, more are needed.

So the cabin will be retired,
Dismantled by a giant dozer
And carted off to a landfill.
In its place will rise two new cabins,
One for me, a second for my sister.

It's just wood and glass and fabric,
I tell myself. Fifty years of family memories
Can't be erased and placed in a dumpster.
Memories live on in our hearts and minds.

Dad died fifteen years ago;
His straw fishing hat still rests on the fireplace mantle.
Mom passed two years ago;
Her lake clothes hang in the bedroom closet undisturbed,
As though she might walk in at any moment.

I'll miss our little cabin.
The sound of the screen door slamming shut,
Followed by mom's voice,
"Don't slam the door!"

The wood frame screen door was salvaged from
    the dump,
As was the wood-fired cook-stove.
I'll miss that too and the smell of pancakes cooking,
The cast iron surface fueled by the wood I split.

Mom decorated the cabin in the early seventies,
Lots of orange and green.
I'll miss the orange padded breakfast bar
     Uncle Joe built
And the orange-green blend shag carpet throughout.

So many years have passed,
The cabin never having been redecorated.
Part of its charm I suppose,
Like a camping spot deep in the woods that
     never changes.
Yet everything changes in time, each at its own pace.

For our little cabin, this is the year of change.
Apprehension is in the air;
We've been neighbors with the same dozen or so
     families for generations.
The feel and taste of the community
Will change when we're through.

My parent's grandchildren have grown up
Spending time at the cabin.
Raised with summers at the lake, they too wonder
If future visits will ever feel the same.

We strive to focus on the positive changes.
A new cabin won't have that years old dusty,
     musty aroma.
The water we drink will be treated, from a well,
     not the lake.
Our windows will be clear, not fogged.
There will be more than one bathroom!

The new cabins can be used in winter,
Should we ever feel so adventurous.
We won't have to follow two pages of instructions
For winterizing the water system.

Our extended families can all visit at the same time—
With plenty of room.
Sitting on the front porch,
The view will be as it's always been.

And yet … I wonder.
Can the present ever smell as sweet
As the remembered past?

Old Robinson cabin wood fire cook-stove

Beach Turmoil

He built a boat house,
Near the shore;
Neighbor said it blocked the view,
Would tolerate it no more.

Down came the structure,
Only two years old;
Neighbor wasn't satisfied,
He was told.

The dock must move,
Too near the property line;
A letter from the state
Threatened a fine.

Piles were pulled,
The whole affair moved;
All so the neighbor's mood
Might be soothed.

Beaches were eroding,
The question was why?
Lake encroachments impeding the water
When the lake level was high.

So retaining walls were torn down,
Boulders moved onshore,
In an experiment of sorts
To see the beach restored.

Angry words were exchanged,
Feelings were hurt;
Like the Hatfields and McCoys
Bridges were burnt.

Time passes slowly,
Heals old scars;
Now life is peaceful
In beach, sun—and stars.

Priest Lake sky from Robinson cabin

A Clash of Values

Late summer day,
Warm and breezy,
Took a long walk
Down the old dirt road.

Passing by, you can't help but notice
Small plain cabins,
The kind built by families on weekends,
Mixed in with lodge-style mansions.

Our lake, our slice of paradise,
Has been invaded by serious money—
Some came as kids and retain our lake values—
They are okay.

Others have newly arrived,
Some from foreign lands,
Like California and Seattle,
Perhaps even Spokane.

Some newcomers carry an attitude,
A work hard play hard view of life
And they do it on their terms,
Having little regard for people around them.

Their children terrorize us on jet skis,
Waveboats churn up ocean swells for hours,
Music blasts from oversize speakers,
A genre of profanity-polluted rap.

Little respect,
Not for people, nor property,
They do as they please,
In the name of *fun*.

The forced sale of state lease lots,
Running off families there for generations
In favor of newcomers,
May be an indicator of what lies ahead.

Or perhaps the varied interests,
Professing to love the lake,
Will seek the courage to resolve their differences,
To accept each other in peace.

Reflection of sky off Soldier's Creek at Priest Lake

ACKNOWLEDGEMENTS

A variation of the poem *Sending Linemen Into the Night* appeared in the August 2016, issue of Rural Electric Magazine. Earlier versions of a handful of the poems have appeared in the Priest Lake Chamber of Commerce Visitors Guide and on various Pecky Cox social media sites.

I owe a huge debt of gratitude to my editor Barbara Rostad, a poet in her own right. The collection of poems in this book took form over a period of nearly ten years and Barbara was involved throughout that time through critique groups and as my editor. This work would be a mere shadow of what it is now without her involvement and guidance.

The North Idaho Writer's League in Coeur d'Alene, Idaho and its predecessor, the Idaho Writer's League – Coeur d'Alene chapter, has been a continual source of support and encouragement as I have worked on this collection of poems. Through their regularly scheduled meetings and critique sessions I have received invaluable input and direction. Without this organization's support this poetry book would have never been written.

I owe a debt of appreciation to the late Larry Telles, who encouraged me to submit the manuscript to Bitterroot Mountain Publishing House where he served on the Board of Directors. Thank you also to John Gessner of Bitterroot Mountain Publishing House, who was assigned as my mentor on this book. John has been supportive of my North Idaho poetry through the entire ten year journey. And a special thank-you to Sarah Vail, also with Bitterroot and the author of several novels, who helped push this book over the finish line.

A huge thank you to Kim Chaffin, my neighbor at Priest Lake, who took the time to beta read the manuscript before I submitted it for publication. She is the author of *Simply Blessed*. There's a poem about her dogs in my book's Dogs of Sherwood Beach section. Her family has been visiting Priest Lake even longer than mine.

And thank you to my Mead High School English and Journalism teacher Mrs. Brookhart, who helped instill and grow in me a love for creative writing.

Finally, I would like to express my thanks to the Priest Lake Museum for allowing me to use many of their archive photographs in the book. And thank you too, to my family and local Priest Lake photographers who offered their pictures for inclusion in this work.

PHOTO CREDITS

Page	Poem/Photo Credit/Description
Cover	Josh Hutchinson, Fuji X-T4 with 16 mm f/1.4, Milky Way over Soldier's Creek Bridge
Map	Priestlaker.com provided the map; location tags by Nate Marrs
3	Introduction, photo credit: Robinson family album, Robinson family dock, September 2017
9	Time, photo credit: Robinson family album, Soldier's Creek Bridge
11	Lake Cabin Limbo Land, photo credit: Robinson family album, original Robinson cabin
16	As Time Wastes Away, photo credit: Robinson family album, Reflection on Priest Lake
21	Sandy at Fifteen, photo credit: Robinson family album, Sandy and Natalie Robinson
31	The Builder's Dog, photo credit: Taila Wachter, Harley
37	Exercising the Labs, photo credit: Robinson family album, Wilson on family beach
40	Dock Girl, photo credit: Robinson family album, Bishop's marina gas dock
43	Ghosts of Girlfriends Past, photo credit: Robinson family album, Robinson cabin
46	Summer Love of '74, photo credit: Robinson family album, Robinson dock

48	A Teen's Lake Romance, photo credit: Kristen Winn, Priest Lake fire pit
51	The Bonfire, photo credit: Robinson family album, beach fire
53	Girl Next Door, photo credit: Priest Lake Museum, Elkins cabin
55	She Loved the Lake, photo credit: Robinson family album, sunset at Priest Lake
57	Déjà vu, photo credit: Eleanor Hungate Jones, fog at Priest Lake
62	Sailing's Inner Peace, photo credit: Kevin Brusett, Author sailing on Priest Lake
66	Sailing Sandy, photo credit: Robinson family album, Sandy on Robinson beach
75	Spring Chill, photo credit: Kristen Winn, chair, cat and fireplace in Priest Lake cabin
77	Seasons, photo credit: Robinson family album, Robinson boat shed
79	Opening the Cabin, photo credit: Robinson family album, Robinson dock
81	Memorial Weekend, photo credit: Robinson family album, Turner walking on Steamboat Bay Road
84	Fall has arrived at the Lake, photo credit: Robinson family album, Robinson beach
88	Sending Linemen Into the Night, photo credit: Kootenai Electric Cooperative, crews working a winter storm
90	Winter Lake Visit, photo credit: Priest Lake Museum, Nell Shipman's sled dogs on the ice with Lloyd Peters sitting on sled. On bottom of photo is written 'Mr. Peters wrote book.' From 8x10 photograph in Leonard Paul photo album

93	The Woodpecker, photo credit: Eleanor Hungate Jones, woodpecker at Priest Lake
97	A Flock of Geese, photo credit: John Renshaw, geese at Priest Lake dock
99	The Hornet Hive, photo credit: Joyce Wilkens, hornet hive at Priest Lake
101	Boy's Fishing Trip, photo credit: Priest Lake Museum, catch at Hunt Creek
108	Sharing a Cabin, photo credit: Robinson family album, Author raking in spring
112	College Beer Run, photo credit: Kristen Winn, boat on Priest Lake at sunset
113	The Lake's Call, photo credit: Robinson family album, highway sign in Priest River
125	Teardown Cabin, photo credit: Robinson family album, original Robinson cabin
127	She Was Ninety-three, photo credit: Robinson family album, Chickie Robinson and family
131	Family Legacy, photo credit: Robinson family album, new cabins on Robinson Sherwood Beach
135	Camp Robinson Golden Anniversary, photo credit: Robinson family album, old cabin's wood stove
137	Beach Turmoil, photo credit: Robinson family album, Priest Lake sky from Robinson cabin
139	A Clash of Values, photo credit: Robinson family album, Soldier's Creek

ABOUT THE AUTHOR

Terry Robinson is an award-winning author and published poet. He is the Idaho Writer's League 2017 Poet of the Year. Terry splits his time between Priest Lake, Idaho and Colorado Springs, Colorado. He spends his days writing poetry and polishing his debut novel. When not writing, Terry can be found hanging out with his grandchildren or playing with his golden retriever Max.

www.ingramcontent.com/pod-product-compliance
Lightning Source LLC
Chambersburg PA
CBHW040804150426
42813CB00056B/2642